With Hope

Morgan
Miller

Hope Stored In Heaven

HOPE AND HEALING THROUGH THE
SORROW OF LOSS AND TRAMA

Morgan Fuller

Table of Contents

Foreword

Our spiritual daughter, Morgan has written an incredible book about overcoming tragedy. So many people get stuck in life because they don't know how to navigate past tragedy. It's always sad to see people walk through tough times but it's even worse when they get stuck in a situation or circumstance. I know that this powerful gem of a book will be used as a tool in the hand of God to help so many. I'm so glad that Morgan penned her story and didn't hold back, because of this, others will be able to walk in freedom.

Joe Joe & Autumn Dawson

Founders and Apostolic Oversight of ROAR Apostolic Network and ROAR Church Texarkana

Introduction

Y ou know those moments, those heart-wrenching moments that change your life completely? The moments that knock the wind out of you and show you what you are really made of? It was one of those moments where time stood still and my faith was tested, a moment forever seared in my memory that I am getting ready to share with you.

I am going to share my journey through healing with you. And because I have no reason to lie to you, it is truly a journey. There is no easy fix, no wake up one morning and everything is all better. It takes time, courage, and a lot of trusting Our Father. Know this though, healing is available to you, if you are willing.

I plan to share all of the heartbreaking details of miscarriage. The sadness, the pain, grief, unworthiness, and the brokenness. But please stick around for the joy, the restoration, the love, and the promise of God fulfilled. I will show you how faithful Our God is and that He never leaves us broken. I am going to share with you the hope stored in Heaven.

Chapter One

Broken But Loved

I grew up in a typical American household. Contrary to popular belief that is not two parents with two and a half kids and a dog. The typical American family is a blended one, with children growing up in homes where their biological parents are divorced and remarried. Kids travel back and forth from Mom's house to Dad's house, have two different bedrooms, sometimes sharing that room with siblings, and basically living two totally different lives from one house to the next.

I was a statistic. I lived one way at one home and another at the other. Things that were acceptable at Dad's house were not acceptable at Mom's house. So, I adapted. I only asked to do the things I knew were allowed at either house and I learned who to ask according to who would let me. I learned how to get what I wanted, and I took every opportunity.

I was a typical Jezebel, manipulating who I had to in order to get what I wanted or thought I needed. I was starved for attention and would do everything I could to get it. In the absence of my father being in my life the way God designed, I sought attention from boys at school. I did what society told me would get them to love me. Despite being surrounded by a tribe of godly father figures at the church I attended with my mom and the abundance of godly women who called me theirs, I still made the same choices as someone who did not have that kind of support.

I was "That Girl." I was promiscuous. I counted myself as worthless. And most of the guys I chose to give my affections to thought the same. I was lost and I was broken. That was until I had a real encounter with Jesus.

You see, until I met Him, I had knowledge of God but no experience. It's like an engineer who designs a bridge. He thinks it will work but until that first vehicle drives across it, he doesn't know for sure.

I had a real encounter with The Father. I was nineteen and had been attending a young adult bible study. I broke up with my current boyfriend, who was living with me at the time because I was convicted of our behavior. I was a half-second away from chasing him down when I received a text message. It was a sound clip of Jeremy Camp's song, "Walk By Faith". You see, I had decided to submit to God, really submit to Him, but my flesh was weak. God knew it. So, He sent someone to strengthen me at just the right time.

Little did I know, the person He chose to use was my future husband, Eric. We were in the same group of friends. In fact, the first time I saw him I remember thinking "that is the most beautiful man I have ever laid eyes on." Then immediately told myself he would never go for a girl like me. He was a godly man, and it was evident in everything he did.

Chapter Two

Marital Bliss Before The Storm

My husband and I married very young. I was just barely twenty years old. Some were overjoyed for us. Some weren't. Some thought we would never make it and others were indifferent about the whole thing. We didn't care. He loved me and I loved him. That's all we needed to know. I didn't have a single doubt in my mind that I was going to spend the rest of my life with Eric Fuller.

I stressed about the rehearsal, the wedding, and the reception. But never once did I stress about saying "I do." Every time I had a complete meltdown during the planning and preparation, Eric was there to bring me back to center.

He is the level head to my high strung, the calm to my storm. He is the easy-going "it will all work out" guy. I am the micromanaging "it all has to be perfect" girl. Every single time he has been there to bring it all back into balance for me, I have loved him more, especially in the days leading up to our wedding.

Right before walking down the aisle my daddy leaned down and whispered, "There is still time to run, my car is just outside." He was joking, of course. In fact, later on down the road, Dad told me he credited watching Eric's life as the spark that lit the desire in him to be a better father, husband, and granddad. To say my husband is one of my greatest blessings would be an understatement, (even if he does drive me batty from time to time).

Eric and I both knew marrying each other was right. I knew God had prepared him just for me. That our life together had so much purpose. What I didn't know was how heavy that mantle could be when we tried to carry it on our own shoulders.

Believe me, when I tell you, it's not any fun at all to carry something you were never meant to. We tried in our own strength and it's never enough. Sometimes, even now we can find ourselves falling back into that old pattern of trying to carry our own burdens. Trust me, my friend, doing what Jesus tells us in The Word and taking His easy yoke and His light burden is the best way. (Matthew 11:30) Everyone can forget sometimes that His shoulders are much better equipped than ours.

Our lives are nothing short of an adventure. And trusting God to help us live it is the best decision we have made together. We have had our share of difficulties and I'm sure there will be more to come. But I can promise you this, we haven't, and we will never let them break us. Not with Holy Spirit at the center of our lives.

On our first wedding anniversary, we not only moved from a one-bedroom apartment to a three-bedroom house, but we were also expecting our firstborn, Rhylee Jane. She is lively, loud, and wild. I wouldn't have her any other way. She keeps me on my toes and all that spirit will thrust her into her purpose! She is going to change the world!

As young parents, we made decisions for our family that we felt, with God's leading, were the very best. We moved churches and joined a church we stayed at for several years. We grew together and worshiped together. We didn't know it at first, but we found a family there that would walk through some of our hardest times with us. Literally, holding us up when we couldn't stand for ourselves. Surrounding us in prayer, support, and love. We found our tribe there.

Chapter Three

Surprise and Tragedy

Life was good and as far as we were concerned it was only getting better. We had a big vision and great hope for the future. What could possibly bring us down? What was the next best thing God was going to bring into our life? Well, I'll tell you.

We had a positive pregnancy test. An unexpected surprise but we were so excited. Our then 3 year-old was going to be a big sister. She was going to be the best big sister! We could hardly contain our excitement. We started sharing as soon as we found out that we were expecting again. Our families were overjoyed. Everyone was so full of happiness. Life was truly only getting better.

As the weeks leading up to our first appointment passed, we discussed all the things a couple does when preparing to meet and bring home a new life. Will they be a boy or a girl? What will they do for the Kingdom of God? Who will this baby look like? What will we name him or her?

I began to think about how I would like to decorate the nursery. Color palettes, wall hangings, furniture. I thought about all the things I would register for and all the things I wouldn't. I knew more this time around what was useful and what would barely get used at all. I didn't want to waste my money or anyone else's.

My husband and I decided on a name very quickly. This time we were ready with a name before anything else. Our baby's name was River Jude. Boy or girl, we just knew this was the name. Little did we know what this name meant and would continue to carry for the both of us.

The day finally came for our first appointment, our first glimpse of this precious baby growing in my womb. The nurse doing the sonogram pulled us back and started the scan. We see the faintest little heartbeat and our hearts leapt. And then I saw it, the unsettling look on the face of the sonographer. A look of distress that she was working very hard to hide.

You see, I worked at the clinic and knew this woman. I knew something wasn't right. "How far along are you supposed to be?" She asked. I should have been nine weeks, but River was only measuring four weeks and three days. "Maybe you've just miscalculated." But I hadn't. I knew that I hadn't.

She led us back to the waiting room with sonogram pictures of our tiny River baby, my hands shaking, and the strong arm of my husband wrapped around me. I'm sure he knew I would have collapsed on the floor had he not held me up. He has a way of just knowing like that. He was steady and unwavering. I am certainly blessed with a mighty man of God.

When we met with our doctor, she seemed hopeful. Maybe it was just for our sake and if that is the case, I am forever grateful. "Let's do another sonogram in two weeks. We will be able to see more and hopefully, we have just miscalculated how far along you are." Everything was "we" and "us", which looking back on it, just solidified that she was going to walk through this with us. She was reassuring us we were not alone. Or at least trying to. I felt broken, empty, and alone. I had never felt more alone in my entire life.

She told me all the reasons we could have been off on our timeline. A couple of them being, I had just had an IUD removed which would mean my cycle would have still been adjusting when I conceived, or I simply did my math wrong.

We left scared but hopeful. However, we were mostly scared. For the next two weeks, I walked around with a fake smile and fabricated joy pretending everything was fine. You know that old saying "fake it 'til you make it." I thought I hid the tribulation in my heart well but let's be honest, my emotions are always written all over my face. The ones who know and love me best can always see right through the cover-up I try to put on. They didn't let on that they could though. They let me pretend but I was screaming for someone, anyone, to say "I know you aren't ok and that's perfectly fine."

We arrived for our next appointment, but this time fear replaced excitement. True terror consumed me. My heart raced like it was going to explode from my chest and I gripped Eric's hand until my knuckles were white. He never complained. He held my hand in the deafening silence, quiet and strong, he stroked the back of my hand with his thumb and when we went back for the sonogram, he held me tight around my waist.

This time, our sonographer couldn't find a heartbeat. When she looked at us, her eyes were soft, kind, and holding back tears for us. It was devastating. I felt every part of me shatter. I was completely broken. There was nothing I could do to catch my breath or stop the room from collapsing around me. And even though we had such compassionate healthcare providers, that didn't make much of a difference in the moment. All I could feel was the emptiness.

My obstetrician was just as kind and compassionate. She hugged me, told us she was so sorry and everything to expect in the coming months. There was blood work, and sonograms, and all kinds of labs. That there would be pain and blood. A lot of blood. She prescribed pain meds, but those pain meds didn't touch the physical pain and did even less for the emotional distress. Every time I had to have more tests done was a reminder that the life that once was inside of me was now gone. A reminder I would never hold that baby, never rock them to sleep, never hear their first words. I would never see them take their first steps, never drop them off on the first day of kindergarten, and a million other firsts that were gone forever.

I told everyone I was fine. When people asked how I was doing, they didn't want the responsibility of listening to what I was really feeling. They did not want the truth. They simply wanted me to know they loved me and were sympathetic to my pain.

But here is the truth, I was not ok. I was hurting. I was angry. And I was becoming more and more bitter with every moment that passed. Every fake smile, every time I lied and said I was fine, all of it created a volatile environment inside my soul. The aching that consumed me raged on the inside and I was desperate to find anyone who understood. But all I found were stories that glossed over the true trauma of what I was going through.

I began to question my reaction. "Should I really be this broken? All the women who have talked about it act like it's not that traumatic. I feel like it's so much worse than what this article says." But the more I looked. The more I read. It all became too clear that it's just not pretty or "appropriate" to be completely candid with messy emotional stuff. Well, the messy emotional stuff was exactly what I needed. I needed to know all of what culture refused to tell me. No more! I will never again let it be said there is nothing out there that shares the true heart-wrenching trauma of miscarriage. No one should ever have to walk through all of that alone.

You see, I know loss is never easy. However, there is something especially devastating that comes with a miscarriage. Not only have you lost a child and all the wonderful possibilities of that precious life, but the enemy sneaks into your thoughts to create all these self-condemning traps for you to fall in. It just begins with questioning how hard you are taking the loss. Then it morphs into something much uglier. You begin to have thoughts like:

"How much of a woman are you if you can't even carry a child for your husband?"

"God must be punishing you for something."

"You don't deserve to be a mother."

These were just a few of the thoughts planted in my mind. Words screaming and tormenting me and so many others who have walked through the same process, the same painful journey.

Chapter Four

Do What You Know Until You Know Better

While I was enduring this tragedy, I was admittedly a very immature Christian. I had been a Christian for a long time but knew very little when it came to life application. I had knowledge but no wisdom. The only scripture I knew by heart outside of John 3:16 was 1 Peter 5:7, which says, "Pour out all your worries and stress upon Him and leave them there, for He always tenderly cares for you."

So, that is exactly what I did. I turned the worship music up as loud as it would go and laid on the floor before God. I laid on my floor crying, screaming, and asking Him, "Why me? Why my baby?"

Well, it was more like demanding answers to my questions. I am so thankful that God is so loving in His response to us even when we are throwing a temper tantrum. I can tell you I was outright awful, and He answered me anyway. Even when He answered me, I was still responding to Him from a place of anger and hurt feelings. God only answered me lovingly and tenderly. He knew exactly how fragile I was and took care to handle my emotions for exactly what they were. That's how faithful Our Father is.

He doesn't always answer us right away. That was certainly the case for me in this. But waiting on The Lord is all I knew to do. So, in the midst of crippling physical pain and excruciating emotional turmoil, I waited. It's funny how teachers can tell you what you should do in hard circumstances, but it never really clicks until you are in the trenches and what they told you is your only option. Just to be clear, when I say I was waiting on The Lord, I don't mean waiting patiently and quietly.

In fact, for several weeks I was impatient, demanding, and bitter. I felt like Job sitting in the ashes. All I could do was cry. I wallowed in my misery and pain. And when I tell you pain, I don't mean just emotional anguish, I mean literal, physical pain.

The day I finally miscarried. The day my body finally released the tiny remains of my River baby I reached for the pain meds my doctor prescribed. She had said "you will need these. Don't refuse to use them when you do." She was right. Two Toradol and a Hydrocodone didn't touch it. And there was so much blood. Even though my doctor told me there would be a lot of blood, I guess I didn't really understand how much blood there would be. And the articles I read simply glossed over the magnitude. I will not be guilty of glossing over this because it was shocking. It shook me to my core, and I was shaking like a leaf in a windstorm. It looked like a murder scene and it felt like one, too. I felt like I was completely discarding my own child even as I grieved the loss of them. It was by far the worst part of the process outside of the moment we heard no heartbeat.

I moped around for weeks after that. Sulked and pouted like a spoiled and selfish child. Angry and broken in the middle of my situation. But I remember when I finally heard Him speak. I was watching a Doris Day film, "Send Me No Flowers", that a friend had loaned to me. I was just trying to think about anything else when God interrupted me. I will never forget it. I had to pause the movie and listen again. He said, "What does River's name mean?"

Immediately I was on the defensive. "I don't want to deal with this right now! I am still angry with you!" I remember thinking to myself. How many of us know God already knew that and He wasn't worried one bit about waiting until I felt like thinking about what was hurting me? He knew better than me. Funny enough, I wanted answers but when presented with the opportunity to get them, I didn't want to do the work.

He repeated again, "What does River's name mean?" Reluctantly, I went and looked up the meaning of my River's name. All the while questioning and mumbling to myself "What does this have to do with anything? River Jude was just a name we liked. This is absolutely ridiculous."

If anyone had been privy to that moment, they would have thought I had lost my mind.

I can just imagine them thinking "Who is she talking to? She must have finally snapped. She's lost it!"

Nonetheless, I went about doing what I felt The Lord had asked of me. And do you know what I found? Obviously, River means "a river". I knew that. I did however learn that "Jude" means "praise." So, the name River Jude meant "A river of praise." I was not amused, nor did I understand what that had to do with anything other than making me think once again about the deep cavity in my chest and emptiness of my womb.

"Okay, so now what? I know what the name means. What am I supposed to do with it?" I was still bitter, still angry, and every bit of my response to The Father was laced with my hurt and bitterness.

I continued to feel the gentle prodding to go deeper, search more, to ask "what does praise mean? What is the purpose of praise?"

For days, I studied on praise and worship. Mostly for something, anything to keep my mind from spiraling into the dark. I have had issues with self-harm and depression in the past and knew it was a slippery slope backward if I didn't dig my heels in and fight. I was hurting and broken but I was not willing to go back to Egypt.

It was in reading 2 Chronicles 20 that I began to receive some clarity. I finally began to understand what God was pointing me toward by asking me what my baby's name meant.

You see, in 2 Chronicles 20, we find King Jehoshaphat crying out to God and getting direction on how to fight a particular battle against a massive enemy. And what did God tell him to do? He told the king to send the worshipers out first! When Israel moved toward battle with the Ammonites, Moabites, and the people of Mount Seir, they advanced under the sound of great praise to God.

Chapter Five

Praise Is A Mighty Weapon

Do you know how that battle ended? Of course, you may know the people of God were victorious, but do you know the extent of their victory? God's people never had to lift a single weapon other than their worship.

When they topped the hillside to look upon their enemies, God's people saw a battlefield of dead enemies. DEAD. Not a single one of their enemies remained alive to challenge them. And just to show how exceedingly and abundantly God answers prayer, the spoils of war were the riches of the three nations that had come against them! How is that for a win, huh?

That was when I understood how powerful praise really is, but I still didn't know why it mattered that praise was a part of River's name. Then I heard God speak to my heart again. For the first time in weeks, I was listening for Him. I wanted to hear from Him.

"He didn't take your praise from you. It's stored in Heaven where he can never touch it again."

Now admittedly, I was confused. I was not worried about my praise. I was hurting because Satan had taken my child from me. I know it would have been really easy to blame God. Very simple to accuse Him of taking my baby but I understood enough about God to know that He gives good gifts and even though He brings good out of the bad, He was not the one who took my child from me. Even so, I didn't understand what God was trying to tell me.

In the meantime, of mulling this over and over in my head, my cousin and his wife had to bury their newborn son. I attended the service intent on being a support to them in such a tragic time, but I was ill-prepared for what would take place. The first note of the first song played and I was broken.

I'm so thankful I was not alone in my seat or sitting next to a stranger because I'm sure they would not have appreciated the puddle I had become all over their shoulder. Ms. Linda Matthews, a dear family friend, was the soft place I needed. God put her there just for me. I fell apart and she held me tight while I lost all my composure. I couldn't plaster the fake smile on my face. I could no longer hold back the tears and it was all I could do to keep from weeping out loud and disrupting the service for a precious baby boy we all hoped to watch grow up. She was immovable and strong when I was a complete and total mess. It was needed and I will always be grateful.

My cousin stood up and spoke at his own child's funeral and that was when it all came together for me. Like a key turning over a lock, I understood exactly what God meant when He told me my praise was stored in Heaven. To quote my cousin he said "I'll never see my son walk but he is dancing on streets of gold. I will never hear his first word, but he is singing with angels today. He may have never opened his eyes here, but the first face he saw was the face of Jesus."

River Jude, my river of praise, was face to face with Jesus. My river of praise was dancing on the streets of gold. My praise, my mighty arrow, my weapon of warfare, was forever stored in Heaven where it will not rust, wither, or die. Stored in Heaven where it can never be taken from me again and one day, I'll see them, hold them, rock them, and kiss them. One day, I'll get to sing with them, dance with them, and hold them with no limit of time.

I finally got it. I finally understood. Satan thought he could take this child from me and I would be powerless to fight anything else he chose to throw at me. He thought I'd be powerless, weak, and easy prey. He was WRONG!

Praise is our mightiest weapon and if I had no desire to praise, I would be without defense and without hope. I was hurting, angry, and broken but I had made up my mind that I would continue to praise God. God, who had taken that tiny child and brought them home with Him. God, who was keeping my River baby safe until I could wrap my arms around them. My weapon was alive, well, and able to withstand whatever Satan formed against me. His weapons would not prosper. My praise and my hope were stored in Heaven with The Father. It was unshakable and unbroken. It was a weapon that would not fail because it is in the hand of The Almighty God.

Chapter Six

Moving Forward With A New Perspective

Now, was I completely healed, and no sorrow left within me at this moment? No. I was not. I still grieve, even today, when I think of all the missed memories with River. But now, I do not grieve without hope and I do not slip into the darkness of despair. Now, I grieve and praise God that this depression is not forever.

This revelation is where the healing started. This was the moment I knew My Father in Heaven had not forsaken me. He had heard me, and He loved me. I was fully confident that My God was looking after me. Day by day, He was healing me.

The dark and heavy feelings would try to creep in. Depression lurked behind every pregnant momma and baby I saw. Misery piped up to be heard every time someone who had also miscarried expressed their condolences. But now, since the revelation of where and with who my River baby was, I had a weapon to war with.

I would remind myself, sometimes multiple times a day, "I have not lost a child. My child is a resident of Heaven. And when I get there, River Jude is going to meet me at the gates."

Am I saying that's all it took to change my mood? Absolutely not. But it did make hope's voice louder than the darkness and that made all the difference.

I was learning that healing is a process. Sometimes you have to be healed as you go. When you learn this, you begin to understand as I did, the brokenness you feel will be healed. You also learn that in order to receive healing you have to expose those vulnerable, broken places to Holy Spirit. I had to, no matter how much it hurt, let God touch the painful places that needed restoration.

Chapter Seven

A Promise And A Made-Up Mind

Often, with me, God speaks in dreams. This particular time it was through a dream I had before. Several times before in fact. You see, I've had this dream multiple times since high school. And maybe it was all for the purpose of leading me to healing at this particularly broken time. This dream has always been exactly the same.

Two little brunette boys. Twins. Running down a hallway into a living room and then jumping into the lap of my grandfather. My mother's father. All three of them laughing big belly laughs.

That's it. That's the whole dream. I always wake up to the sound of their laughter. But, this time, it was different. Holy Spirit spoke to me when I awoke. He said, "Your last experience as an expectant mother will not be loss."

Now, if that isn't a word you can war with, I don't know what is! That was a promise I could hold onto. It was mine. Specifically spoken out of Heaven for me. When Heaven gives you a promise, nothing can change your mind. Nothing can make you doubt that you are going to receive it.

There were people who I loved and loved me dearly but as the time stretched on they doubted and even questioned my ability to hear God.

"Are you sure that's what He said?"

"Did you hear that for yourself or did some-one else tell you?"

"What if you're wrong?"

You see, I learned that I didn't need anyone else to believe my promise for me. I knew My Father's voice and I could believe Him even if I had to believe Him all by myself.

If God gives you a promise it is YOUR JOB to hold it tight and continue to trust Him for it. No one else can hold it for you. No one else will understand the magnitude of what it means for you. They may mean well but the enemy is great at using the voices of those who love us to create doubt in us. Don't be angry with them, go to war against the enemy. Fight with the promise God gave you. It will not fail.

Choose to replace the voice of the enemy with the voice of truth. Instead of listening to the voice saying, "Are you sure that's what God said?" Remind yourself of Jesus' words in John 10:14, "The Word says "I alone am the Good Shepherd, and I know those whose hearts are Mine, for they recognize Me and know Me."

When you hear Satan tell you "You couldn't be a good parent, that's why God took that baby from you." Tell yourself "God gives good gifts and equips us to hold what He has for us. I am well able because Christ makes me able."

For some scriptures to stand on look at these:

"Every gift God freely gives us is good and perfect, streaming down from the Father of lights, who shines from the heavens with no hidden shadow or darkness and is never subject to change." James 1:17

"For in reality, the power we have is used in support of the truth, not against it. And we claim before God that you will be fully equipped and mature, for it brings us great joy when you are strong, even if we seem weak and denigrated." 2 Corinthians 13:8-9

"Jesus looked at them and replied, "With people it is impossible, but not with God—God makes all things possible!" Mark 10:27

When you pair The Word with praise, you have an UNSTOPPABLE weapon against the plans of the enemy. You have an UNSHAKABLE foundation. And, when you do this you will be strengthening your faith in your UNDEFEATED Defender!

Chapter Eight

It's All A Matter Of Time

Through the years I have clung to the promise of another child, sometimes as if my life depended on it. When doubt tried to creep in, which was often. I wouldn't let it be one that I forgot. I refused to drop my promise by the wayside just because I didn't see it come to fruition quickly enough. I knew my Father's voice and I was holding tightly to the word He spoke to my heart.

That's all I could do.

Hold on.

Wait.

I had to cling to my still longed for promise.

You see, God isn't trapped in time like we are. He told me what He was going to do and that was it. But there in the waiting was where my resolve was tested. It was where my faith was tested. Did I believe God or not? Did I trust Him or not?

And you know what, more than anything else, I believed God. I trusted Him. He had always been faithful to everything He had ever told me. Naming those things He had come through on was another weapon in my arsenal during the waiting. What reason did I have to doubt that He would come through on this too? I made up my mind that no matter who doubted my promise, I would see it fulfilled. My promise would be kept, and it would be a testimony of His goodness. A reminder to every one of just how faithful God is.

My friend, He is so very faithful. God watches over His word to see it completed. He will see to it that every word He has spoken to you comes to pass. You just have to stay the course and trust Him.

I know, you're thinking "Well that's a lot easier said than done". You're right. It is. But nobody ever said (and was telling the truth) that living this life was all sunshine and rainbows. In fact, The Word tells us to continue to rejoice in our sufferings. Don't believe me? Just read this in 1 Peter 4:13, "Instead, continue to rejoice, for you, in a measure, have shared in the sufferings of the Anointed One so that you can share in the revelation of His glory and celebrate with even greater gladness!"

How is that for encouragement? Yes, I'm telling you that you will face hard times, struggles, and sometimes even true suffering. But you do not face them without hope or without a Father to walk with you! A Father who is faithful to keep His word. I know so because I have lived to the fruition of His fulfilled promise!

Chapter Nine

Process To The Promise

For five very long years, I held onto the promise of another child. I clung to it. I gripped it tight in my heart and refused to let it slip away. I knew what God had told me and I was not about to let anyone convince me otherwise. So, it stands to reason I would be overjoyed when I found out I was expecting, right?

WRONG! SO WRONG!

I was stunned. I was in denial. In fact, for a week I was complaining to my friend at work about feeling nauseous and could not figure out why. She finally looked at me and said "Morgan, you're pregnant." To which I responded with a very certain "No, I am not!"

Then, I looked at the calendar. I was 12 days late. All I could think about were the reasons why this was not the right time for this promise to come. How funny and somewhat tragic is it that so often we wait and wait for our promise and then when it comes, we are utterly unprepared?

I was not at all ready.

But I went home and took a test. Actually, I took three. And all three of them had a shocking positive result. I was stunned and afraid. How was I going to tell Eric? We were not prepared for this!

Nothing was ideal. We were not in our own space. Our finances were not what we thought they should be. We had a huge trip planned for around the estimated due date, etc.

Sad, isn't it? When you get what you've been praying for only to realize you now have to be ready when you should have already been ready. It's sad but it was my reality. I had failed to prepare for my promise.

I had done everything else. I spoke life over my promise. When doubt and despair tried to creep in, I reminded myself (and every demon that tried to deceive me) what My Father had said. I even bought a few little baby items along the way. But I was utterly under prepared to actually hold my promise.

In fact, I made a lab appointment to confirm because I was so unsure. I was definitely pregnant. I was carrying my promise. My dear friend, Michelle, worked at our oldest daughter's school and when I got there to pick RJ up, I looked at Michelle in disbelief and told her I was expecting. She was the first person I told outside of Eric. I was stunned. I'm sure she could tell you I looked every bit as shocked as I felt.

It was surreal. I walked around dazed with shock for a good week or so. The process of becoming excited was so surprisingly difficult.

I knew I was carrying my promise. I knew in just a short time I would hold my promise in my arms. I knew God had been true to the promise He made to me five years prior. But I was overwhelmingly fearful.

What women who have children after a miscarriage often forget to tell you is that anxiety and hyper-vigilance tries to consume you. Fear tries to suck every ounce of joy out of the entire experience of living in the promise fulfilled.

Fear whispers in your ear, "What if it happens again?"

"Will you get to hold this baby?"

"How do you know you won't miscarry again?"

To make all those thoughts so much harder to fight, I had some small (but really big to me) issues during this pregnancy.

I had many occasions of spotting and bleeding. One, in particular, that had me trembling uncontrollably and gripped tightly by fear.

I had gotten up to go to the restroom. Eric was on his way home from work. He was working the night shift at the time. There was a lot of blood and I immediately began to panic. I called him and told him we had to go to the hospital. Eric's dad was just getting up as well and he hugged me tight and began to pray. I was shaking so hard and trying to hold it together at the same time.

I was simultaneously terrified that I was miscarrying again, trying not to panic, and feeling guilty for the stress I was possibly putting on the baby in what could already be a bad situation. Talk about fear and anxiety having their way with me.

I was so scared. I couldn't even call our Apostle because I knew I wouldn't be able to get the words out. I sent him and his wife a text to ask them to pray for us and let him know what was going on.

Well, let me tell you, you need good leaders in your life. You need leaders who get in the trenches with you. That's exactly what they did, too. Joe showed up at the emergency room shortly after they took me back. He stayed for a little while and prayed with us. They continued to pray with us. Autumn checked on us. The support we had, have always had, and continue to receive from them is exactly what I feel strong, godly leaders should be doing. They are family and we are so very blessed to be running this race with them.

I wish I could tell you that God took all my fear away and I didn't struggle with this long. But I promised not to lie to you or sugar-coat the truth. I struggled and fought with fear and anxiety throughout the entire pregnancy.

It was a constant effort to take every thought captive and to filter my emotions properly. It was a daily task to evaluate and reframe what was true. Many times a day I had to remind myself of God's promises to me and what He created the female body to do.

I would speak things over myself and our baby to keep my mind focused on the truth.

Daily affirmations that became so ingrained in my spirit that when these moments of struggle presented, I had something to war with.

Here are a few if you ever need them:
I am a capable woman (Taken from
    Proverbs 31)
I do not submit to fear
My mind is ruled by and filled with the
    spirit of peace
My God keeps His promises

And the one I used most often that My Apostle's wife spoke over me from the very first complication: "I was created to conceive, carry, and deliver this baby."

That statement carries so much weight! Understand this. God created the female form not just to conceive, not just to conceive and carry, but to conceive, carry, AND deliver babies. It also declares to the enemy "THIS baby, the one in my womb right now, will not come until it's appointed time. "

My friend Lorna also shared an affirmation with me out of scripture that she herself warred with for her baby.

"My vine will not drop its fruit until it is time" (taken from Malachi 3:10-11).

I'm not saying these words saved my baby, but I am saying your mindset does a lot for the atmosphere you live in. Your thoughts and words shape your world. They are weapons against the enemy of fear and anxiety. You must learn to FIGHT BACK, or you will SHRINK BACK!

If I can give you anything in this chapter, I want it to be this. It's ok to admit you're struggling and it's ok to have emotions. You just have to be willing to fight your way out of there. You have to choose to use the weapons God has given you (promises, scripture, and the power in your words) to stay in the fight and not be consumed by the enemy that is whispering in your ear. Don't give in. Our Father is faithful to keep His word.

Chapter Ten

Suffering In Silence

One thing I have learned about myself is I am constantly allowing myself to believe I am a burden to my friends and family if I reach out for help. I am the listener, the counselor, the helper, the peacemaker. I love being those things but along with that part of myself is the wrong mindset that it will make too many waves if I am the one needing the support.

I cannot tell you how many times I told myself "Don't text them about this. They don't have time for you." or "It's not a big enough issue to warrant asking them to pray."

That is a LIE straight from the pit of hell sent to keep me isolated and suffering alone! And I am certain it is one the enemy uses on so many like me.

Satan wants more than anything to isolate and silence the church and he will use any method necessary to do it. He knows if he can keep you quiet about your suffering, you can't wake any more of God's children up to ask Daddy God to do anything about your situation with you.

I want to encourage you here. Wake up some kids! Get some Brothers and Sisters who will knock on the doors and windows of Heaven with you. Find you an Aaron and Hur to hold your arms up when you are tired.

Suffering in silence was one of the worst mistakes I made during the pregnancy carrying our rainbow baby.

Yes, I leaned into The Father, but He created people for community because we NEED each other. We need people to walk with us, cry with us, and pray with us. If you are going through anything, not just miscarriage or a pregnancy following a miscarriage, ANYTHING at all, DO NOT believe the lie that you are a burden to your friends and family. I'm sure if you asked them, they would tell you this "You are not a burden to us. We want to pray with you and help you through this."

Please, do not suffer in silence.

Thankfully, I had friends who did this very thing for me. They continually reassured me I was not a bother or burden. They were available when I was in the midst of a fear-induced panic. They held my hands and warred with me when complications arose. I told you earlier, we found our tribe. Our tribe loves and wars with a God-given fierceness. Eric and I knew before long that we had people in our corner who wanted to be in our corner. They didn't feel obligated. They didn't feel like we were a burden. They loved us and our family and they were with us every step of the way.

Friend, find your tribe.

Chapter Eleven

Favored And Well-Known

Among the many confirming words along this five-year journey, a few dreams, and a few personal encounters with Holy Spirit, I knew our son would be named Joshua Gideon. And one thing I just knew when I got over the shock of finding out we were in fact expecting is that we were having a boy. "My promise is for Joshua. We are having a boy. I am certain."

Imagine my surprise when the sonographer tells me this child is a GIRL! Now, please don't think I was disappointed. I was overwhelmed with joy that she looked perfect on that sonogram. Everything was as it should be and there were no signs of anything out of sorts. The wave of relief at that cannot be described with words.

For me, this was simple. We had been given, actually, the word was given to Eric by our Apostle's Apostle, Ken Malone. Apostle Ken didn't know us at this point. He had only met us once. He asked Eric if he had children to which Eric responded "One." Apostle Ken looked at Eric and said, "Get ready because I see three".

I can count, Friend. I promise, I really can, I know Rhylee, River, and this baby make three. So, I had to be mistaken in having heard The Lord tell me the name, Joshua Gideon. Lord knows plenty of people pointed that out. But remember what I told you earlier?

You don't need anyone else's faith to believe for your promise.

Now, let me assure you before we move on, I'm still believing for Joshua to arrive. However, in the meantime, I am enjoying my beautiful, brilliant little girls. I'm still loving being a girl mom. Friend, make no mistake it is absolutely okay to enjoy where you are while waiting on your future. Don't let any lie of the enemy convince you otherwise. We have to be content with where we are in the journey and appreciate all the wonderful things we have in the present.

We were having a girl and she was healthy. She had all ten fingers and all ten toes. Everything was right in the place it was supposed to be. I was absolutely overjoyed at this good news. But now, what in the world were we going to name her?

I had spent so long knowing my son would be named Joshua Gideon that I hadn't even given thought to what we would name another daughter.

There were a few things we knew. We wanted a strong name. We wanted her name to speak to her destiny and have meaning. We didn't want to just name her something we thought was pretty. After our experience with River and the great significance of River's name, we couldn't go back to names that didn't mean something profound to us.

I have always loved old names, So I suggested names like Evangeline (which means evangelist) and Josephine (which means dreamer). Eric would have none of that. He insisted he wanted a simple name. Easy to spell and still significant.

The time for her to arrive kept getting closer and we still could not agree on anything. We got close though. We both liked the name Claire, which means "well known", Eric kept coming back to the name Anna, which means "favored by The Lord". But I didn't want something as short as just Anna. So, I suggested we hyphenate her first name. Anna-Claire. Then we could have one of the names I wanted as a middle name.

I mean, Anna-Claire Josephine would mean "Favored and well-known dreamer"! How perfect is that?

Eric shot it down and I just could not understand why he couldn't compromise. So, I did what any good Christian wife does. I complained to...I mean, asked God to work on my husband's unbending attitude.

Funny how I still haven't learned that God more often wants to deal with my attitude when I talk to Him rather than someone else's.

One afternoon I am driving down the street, once again advising God on how to deal with my husband about this baby-naming business, when God asks me a question that I have to pull over for. He said to me "Why does she have to be favored and well known for just one thing?"

Talk about an attitude adjustment! Here I was arguing with God to limit my child's destiny to just one thing. Of course, I didn't realize that's what I was doing at the time. Why couldn't she be favored and well known for many things? What great things does He have planned for her life? I couldn't argue with that.

So, two weeks before her due date, we finally had her name, Anna Claire, meaning favored and well-known by The Lord. You can't really have a more powerful and purposeful name than that.

Chapter Twelve

A Rainbow Shines

Eric was back working day shifts by the time Anna made her grand entrance into the world, but he was still adjusting to the shift change. The night before I went into labor, he had to take a sleep aid just to get some sleep. Poor thing. About 2:30 a.m. I woke up feeling a bit of discomfort, but I wasn't sure if it was contractions or not. You see, with our eldest, RJ, I had been induced so it was a totally different experience. So, I laid in bed awake trying to determine if this was real or just my body preparing for labor down the road. At about 3:45 am, I knew for sure this was early labor, so I got up and paced the dining room to manage the discomfort of the contractions. I wanted to let Eric sleep as long as I could because he was finally getting to rest. I was also attempting to hold back the feeling of jealousy every time I heard him snore.

I went back and forth from pacing the dining room to trying to lay down and doze between contractions. They were about 12 to 15 minutes apart at the time, so I knew there was no rush to head to the hospital. This went on for what seemed like forever. I knew it wasn't though. My father-in-law got up each morning at about 5:15. So when his alarm went off and he went to the living room I got out of bed and into the shower. The pain in my lower back was starting to get intense and I was hoping hot water would help ease it.

I was right. It did for about 45 minutes. When I got out of the shower, I realized there was a problem getting dry. My water had broken. No, It wasn't like in the movies where there is this big gush and a mess on the floor. Apparently, more often it's just a trickle. But once your water breaks, it's time to head to where you are planning to have the baby. I had given Eric all the time I could to sleep.

Once I shook him awake, we packed up the car, installed the car seat, woke RJ up, and made our way to the hospital. It wasn't too far, and we made it there without any issue. On the way, I called my mom who was going to spend the day entertaining and waiting with our daughter. Everyone was excited.

Once at the hospital and settled Eric took another nap and I rested in the bed. Just so you are aware, once your water breaks, they don't let you walk around too much. So, I read and listened to my worship music. Our nurse was fantastic. She made sure I stayed comfortable and she even helped me keep my diffuser going with essential oils that filled the room with comforting smells instead of the sterile smell of hospital cleaners. She was so easy going and she let me, for the most part, labor the way I wanted to labor.

We did a few things differently this go-round.

We only told a few people we were there and we had zero visitors while I was laboring. Last time, I couldn't rest for the feeling of having to be social with everyone who came to check on me. I did not want that this time and I am so thankful we chose to do things this way. It was so peaceful. We also waited until she was born and we had time with her before we allowed anyone else in. Again, one of the best decisions we ever made.

RJ was so proud to be a big sister. All of us were so in love from the first moment we saw her. But the biggest thing for me was the washing away of so much fear and anxiety. I was holding my long-awaited promise! I was overwhelmed by the great goodness of My Father. He had been found faithful once again.

I was not surprised by His faithfulness, but I was in awe of it. The instant I felt the weight of my favored and well-known promise in my arms, the unfathomable peace, and presence of God rushed in and filled up the whole room. A true and complete healing took place in that moment. It is unforgettable and still, all-consuming awe takes hold when I think about God's goodness in that moment.

My rainbow baby had finally made her appearance. Anna Claire was and is a very bright rainbow after such a terrible storm. The healing that I have experienced is one I pray for every mother who has suffered a loss to have. And while everyone's healing comes from different places and in different ways, I know one thing for certain, God's will is always to heal. We just have to submit to the process of healing.

Chapter Thirteen

Parting Encouragement

My Friend, I hope whatever healing you are waiting for that you do not lose hope in the One who promised it to you. I hope that He surrounds you with people who will hold up your arms when you don't have the strength to hold them up yourself.

I pray that you find your tribe that will love you fiercely and will pound on the doors and windows of Heaven for you. I pray you latch on to every promise The Lord gives you and use it to war for your promise when the enemy whispers doubt in your ears. I pray you never forget that while having a tribe is so necessary you only need you to believe for the promises Your Father has given you.

Most of all, I pray you choose to hear Him when He speaks to you. I pray that no matter how angry, hurt, or bitter you may be that you will choose to listen for His whispers. And I pray you never forget that as His child you can hear His voice.

I pray your healing process is one that you are brave enough to share. That you will use it to testify to the goodness of God. I pray that you never lose sight of the promises God has made to you. I pray you are encouraged to hold tight to your promises because you know beyond any doubt that The One who made them is faithful.

Friend, understand that your Father is always for you. He has good things for you, and

He loves you more than you can even begin to imagine.

There is hope. A hope that is stored in Heaven where our enemy cannot touch or take it. It will not rust. It will not wither. Hope will not fade because our hope is found in Jesus.

Until we chat again, I bless you.

Our Journey

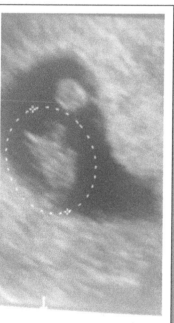

About The Author

Morgan Fuller is happily married to her best friend, Eric Fuller. Together they strive to raise their daughters, Rhylee Jane and Anna Claire, to love and live for Jesus radically and unapologetically. Morgan currently serves on the leadership team for ROAR Church Texarkana and is a member of ROAR Apostolic Network. She desires to see people set free and living wild for the Lord. Her heart's cry is to give voice back to the Church and to declare the goodness of God all the days of her life.

OTHER BOOKS BY MORGAN FULLER

CHAMPIONS ARE FORGED IN FIRE
CRIES OF A WARRIOR

CPSIA information can be obtained
at www.ICGtesting.com
Printed in the USA
FSHW020542051020